The Happiness Mindset for Students: Thriving in Academic and Personal Life

By Hodaya Zehavi with the AI assistance

©2023

D1718639

Contents

Introduction

Welcome to "The Happiness Mindset for Students: Thriving in Academic and Personal Life." In this book, we will explore the power of developing a positive mindset and how it can transform your experience as a student. As a student, you face unique challenges and pressures in both your academic and personal life. It's easy to get caught up in the stress, anxiety, and overwhelm that often accompany the pursuit of education. However, by adopting a happiness mindset, you can navigate these challenges with resilience, find joy in the learning process, and ultimately achieve success on your terms. In this book, we will delve into various topics that will help you cultivate a happiness mindset and create a fulfilling academic journey. From setting goals and building resilience to managing stress and developing healthy habits, each chapter will provide you with practical strategies and insights to enhance your well-being and academic performance.

Throughout this journey, we will draw upon the latest research in positive psychology, neuroscience, and personal development. But don't worry, this book is not just a series of theories and concepts. It is a guide that combines theory with practical techniques and exercises to help you apply these principles in your everyday life. Here's a breakdown of what you can expect in each chapter:

CHAPTER 1: THE POWER OF A POSITIVE MINDSET

Explore the science behind positive psychology and how it can influence your mindset. Discover the benefits of adopting a positive perspective and learn techniques to reframe negative thoughts.

CHAPTER 2: SETTING GOALS FOR SUCCESS

Discover the importance of setting clear and achievable goals, both short-term and long-term. Learn how to set SMART goals and create an action plan to turn your aspirations into reality.

CHAPTER 3: BUILDING RESILIENCE AND BOUNCING BACK FROM FAILURE

Develop resilience skills to overcome setbacks and learn from failures. Explore strategies to build mental toughness, adaptability, and bounce back stronger after experiencing disappointments.

CHAPTER 4: CULTIVATING A GROWTH MINDSET

Understand the difference between a fixed mindset and a growth mindset. Learn how to embrace challenges, persevere through obstacles, and tap into your full potential.

CHAPTER 5: MANAGING STRESS AND ANXIETY

Learn effective techniques to manage stress and anxiety to optimize your overall well-being and academic performance. Explore mindfulness exercises, relaxation techniques, and stress reduction strategies.

CHAPTER 6: THE IMPORTANCE OF SELF-CARE

Recognize the significance of self-care in maintaining a healthy balance between academic demands and personal well-being.

Discover self-care practices that nurture your physical, mental, and emotional health.

CHAPTER 7: DEVELOPING HEALTHY HABITS FOR ACADEMIC SUCCESS

Learn how to cultivate habits that support your academic success. Discover strategies for improving your sleep, nutrition, exercise routine, and overall lifestyle choices.

CHAPTER 8: ENHANCING FOCUS AND CONCENTRATION

Master techniques to enhance your focus and concentration during studying and learning activities. Explore methods to minimize distractions and improve your ability to retain information effectively.

CHAPTER 9: EFFECTIVE TIME MANAGEMENT STRATEGIES

Unlock the secrets of effective time management to optimize your productivity and reduce overwhelm. Learn how to prioritize tasks, create schedules, and make the most of your available time.

CHAPTER 10: OVERCOMING PROCRASTINATION

Understand the underlying causes of procrastination and learn strategies to overcome this common challenge. Discover techniques to increase motivation, set deadlines, and maintain consistency. Stay tuned for the upcoming chapters as we dive deeper into each topic and provide you with practical tools and insights to help you thrive as a student. Remember, cultivating a happiness mindset is a lifelong journey, and your willingness to embrace these concepts and techniques will undoubtedly transform your academic and personal life. Let's embark on this journey together!

Chapter 1: The Power of a Positive Mindset

In this chapter, we will explore the incredible power of a positive mindset and how it can greatly impact your academic and personal life. A positive mindset is not just about thinking happy thoughts; it is a way of approaching life with optimism and resilience.

THE BENEFITS OF A POSITIVE MINDSET

A positive mindset can have numerous benefits for students. Firstly, it helps to enhance your overall well-being and mental health. When you focus on the positive aspects of life and cultivate an optimistic mindset, you are better able to manage stress, anxiety, and other challenges that come your way. Moreover, a positive mindset has a direct impact on your academic performance. Research has shown that students with a positive mindset tend to have higher levels of motivation, engagement, and perseverance. They are more likely to set ambitious goals and work towards achieving them. They also tend to have higher levels of self-confidence and belief in their abilities, which can greatly improve their performance and outcomes.

SHIFTING TO A POSITIVE MINDSET

Developing a positive mindset is not an overnight process; it takes time and effort. Here are a few strategies to help you shift to a positive mindset:

Practice gratitude:

One of the most effective ways to cultivate a positive mindset is by practicing gratitude. Take a few moments every day to reflect on the things you are grateful for. This simple practice can help shift your focus from negativity to positivity.

Challenge negative thoughts:

Negative thoughts can often cloud our minds and hinder our progress. Practice identifying negative thoughts and challenging them with positive affirmations or alternative perspectives. Train your mind to focus on solutions rather than dwelling on problems.

Surround yourself with positivity:

The people and environment you surround yourself with can greatly influence your mindset. Surround yourself with positive and supportive individuals who uplift and inspire you. Create a positive environment by surrounding yourself with motivational quotes, affirmations, and inspiring visuals.

Practice self-compassion:

Be kind and compassionate towards yourself. Acknowledge that setbacks and failures are a part of life, and they do not define your worth or potential. Treat yourself with the same kindness and understanding you would offer to a friend facing similar challenges.

CONCLUSION

Having a positive mindset is a powerful tool that can help you navigate through the ups and downs of academic and personal life. By shifting your mindset and adopting a positive outlook, you can enhance your overall well-being, improve your academic performance, and achieve greater success. In the following chapters, we will explore various strategies and techniques that will further empower you to cultivate and maintain a positive mindset.

Chapter 2: Setting Goals for Success

Setting goals is an essential component of achieving success in both academic and personal endeavors. When you have clear goals in mind, you are more likely to stay motivated, focused, and productive. In this chapter, we will explore the importance of setting goals and provide you with practical strategies to set effective and achievable goals.

THE BENEFITS OF SETTING GOALS

Setting goals allows you to have a clear vision of what you want to accomplish. It provides you with direction and purpose, giving your efforts a sense of meaning. Here are some key benefits of setting goals:

1. Motivation:

When you have a goal in mind, it fuels your motivation and drives you to take action. Goals act as a source of inspiration, pushing you to work hard and overcome obstacles along the way.

2. Focus:

Setting goals helps you focus on what is most important. It helps you prioritize your time, energy, and resources towards activities that align with your desired outcomes.

3. Clarity:

By setting goals, you gain clarity about what you truly want to achieve. It helps you define your objectives and create a roadmap to success.

4. Measurement:

Goals provide a measurable benchmark against which you can assess your progress.

It allows you to track your achievements and make necessary adjustments if needed.

5. Achievement:

Working towards and achieving goals provides a sense of accomplishment and boosts your self-confidence. Each small milestone achieved brings you closer to your ultimate goal, fostering a sense of fulfillment and satisfaction.

STRATEGIES FOR SETTING EFFECTIVE GOALS

While setting goals is crucial, it is equally important to set effective and achievable ones. Here are some strategies to help you set goals that propel you towards success:

1. SMART Goals:

Utilize the SMART goals framework to ensure your goals are Specific, Measurable, Achievable, Relevant, and Time-bound. This approach helps you create goals that are clear, realistic, and have a defined timeline for completion.

2. Break It Down:

Break down your goals into smaller, more manageable tasks and milestones. This not only makes the overall goal less overwhelming but also allows you to celebrate small wins along the way.

3. Prioritize:

Prioritize your goals based on their importance and urgency. Focus on the most critical goals first while keeping in mind long-term objectives.

4. Visualize:

Create a visual representation of your goals, such as a vision board or a written statement. This will serve as a constant reminder of what you are working towards and keep you motivated.

5. Review and Refine:

Regularly review your goals and evaluate your progress. If necessary, refine them to ensure they remain relevant and attainable. Remember, goal-setting is a continuous process. As you accomplish one goal, set new ones to continue challenging yourself and reaching new heights. With a clear and well-defined set of goals, you are laying a solid foundation for long-term success. By setting goals for success, you are taking control of your academic and personal life. So, dare to dream, set ambitious goals, and work diligently towards achieving them. With the right mindset and effective goal-setting strategies in place, you are bound to accomplish great things.

Chapter 3: Building Resilience and Bouncing Back from Failure

Failure is an inevitable part of life. Whether it's receiving a low grade on a test, not getting accepted into a desired program, or facing rejection in a personal relationship, everyone experiences setbacks at some point. The key to success, however, lies in how we respond to these failures and setbacks.

THE IMPORTANCE OF BUILDING RESILIENCE

Resilience is the ability to bounce back from adversity, challenges, and failures. It is a crucial skill for students to develop, as it helps in maintaining motivation, perseverance, and mental well-being. Building resilience allows students to view failures as opportunities for growth rather than as obstacles that define their abilities or limit their potential.

Recognizing the Learning Potential in Failure

One of the first steps in building resilience is to shift our mindset and reframe how we view failure. Instead of viewing failure as a negative outcome, we can choose to see it as a learning opportunity. Every failure is a chance to learn, improve, and grow. By adopting this perspective, students can develop a growth mindset that embraces challenges and sees setbacks as stepping stones toward success.

Developing Self-Compassion

When faced with failure, it's important for students to practice self-compassion. Rather than being overly critical or harsh on themselves, they need to treat themselves with kindness and understanding. Self-compassion involves acknowledging and accepting the failure while also recognizing that everyone makes mistakes. By practicing self-compassion, students can bounce back from failure with resilience and maintain a positive attitude.

Building Supportive Relationships

Having a strong support system is crucial for building resilience. Students should surround themselves with friends, family, teachers, or mentors who provide encouragement, guidance, and understanding. These supportive relationships can help students navigate through failures, offer different perspectives, and provide emotional support during challenging times. By having a network of support, students can gain resilience and bounce back stronger from failures.

Developing Problem-Solving Skills

When faced with failure, it's important to develop problem-solving skills. By taking a proactive approach and analyzing what went wrong, students can identify effective solutions and strategies to overcome future challenges. Problem-solving skills can be developed through brainstorming, seeking advice from others, and learning from past experiences. By focusing on finding solutions instead of dwelling on failures, students can build resilience and improve their ability to bounce back.

PRACTICAL STRATEGIES FOR BOUNCING BACK FROM FAILURE

To effectively bounce back from failure, students can employ several practical strategies: - **Reflect and Learn:** Take the time to reflect on the failure and identify the lessons learned. Understand what factors contributed to the failure and use this knowledge to make improvements for the future. - **Set Realistic Expectations:** Unrealistic expectations can set students up for failure. Setting realistic goals and expectations ensures that students are more likely to achieve success and avoid feelings of disappointment or failure. - **Prioritize Self-Care:** Taking care of one's physical and mental well-being is crucial in building resilience. Engaging in activities like exercise, mindfulness, and hobbies can have a positive impact on mental health and help students cope with failures. - **Seek Support:** Reach out to friends, family, or teachers for support and encouragement. Having someone to talk to and share experiences with can provide a fresh perspective, guidance, and emotional support during challenging times. - **Develop a Growth Mindset:** Embrace failures as opportunities for growth and development. Cultivate a mindset that believes that abilities and intelligence can be developed through hard work, dedication, and perseverance.

CONCLUSION

Building resilience and bouncing back from failure are essential skills for students to thrive in their academic and personal lives. By reframing the way we view failure, practicing self-compassion, building supportive relationships, and developing problem-solving skills, students can foster resilience and turn setbacks into opportunities for growth. Remember, failure is not the end, but rather a stepping stone towards success. Embrace failures, learn from them, and keep moving forward with determination and resilience.

Chapter 4: Cultivating a Growth Mindset

Having a growth mindset is crucial for students as it can significantly impact their academic and personal success. In this chapter, we will explore what a growth mindset is, the benefits it offers, and practical strategies to cultivate this mindset.

UNDERSTANDING THE GROWTH MINDSET

A growth mindset is the belief that intelligence and abilities can be developed through dedication, effort, and learning.

Students with a growth mindset embrace challenges, persist in the face of setbacks, see effort as the path to mastery, and learn from feedback and criticism. On the other hand, a fixed mindset is the belief that intelligence and abilities are set traits, where success or failure is attributed to inherent qualities. Students with a fixed mindset may avoid challenges, give up easily, ignore feedback, and feel threatened by the success of others.

The Benefits of a Growth Mindset

Cultivating a growth mindset has numerous benefits for students. It enhances resilience, motivation, and self-confidence. When students believe that their abilities can improve over time, they become more willing to put in the effort required to achieve their goals. They are also more likely to view challenges as opportunities for growth and learning, rather than insurmountable obstacles. A growth mindset also fosters a love for learning. Students with this mindset are more open to seeking new knowledge, exploring different approaches, and embracing feedback. They understand that setbacks and failures are an integral part of the learning process and use them as stepping stones toward improvement.

DEVELOPING A GROWTH MINDSET

Now that we understand the importance and benefits of a growth mindset, let's explore some practical strategies to cultivate this mindset:

1. Embrace Challenges:

Rather than avoiding challenges, actively seek them out. Challenges provide opportunities for growth and expansion of skills. Embrace the notion that challenges are a natural part of the learning process and are essential for personal and academic growth.

2. Persist in the Face of Setbacks:

View setbacks and failures as valuable learning experiences. Instead of giving up, use them as stepping stones toward success. Embrace the mindset that setbacks are temporary and can be overcome with effort and resilience.

3. Adopt a Growth-Oriented Language:

Be mindful of the language you use when discussing abilities and achievements. Instead of saying, "I can't do this," adopt a growth-oriented approach by saying, "I can't do this yet, but with effort and practice, I will improve."

4. Emphasize Effort:

Focus on the process rather than the outcome. Encourage students to value hard work, dedication, and perseverance. By recognizing and celebrating their effort, students become more motivated to continue striving for improvement.

5. Embrace Criticism and Feedback:

Instead of feeling threatened or defensive when receiving criticism or feedback, see it as an opportunity for growth. Embrace constructive criticism, learn from it, and use it as a catalyst for personal development.

6. Surround Yourself with Growth-Minded People:

Build a supportive network of individuals who share a growth mindset. Surrounding yourself with like-minded people who embrace challenges and view failure as an opportunity for growth will reinforce and strengthen your own growth mindset.

CONCLUSION

Cultivating a growth mindset is essential for students to reach their full potential in both their academic and personal lives. By embracing challenges, persisting in the face of setbacks, adopting growth-oriented language, emphasizing effort, embracing criticism and feedback, and surrounding themselves with growth-minded individuals, students can cultivate a mindset that promotes continuous learning and personal development.

CHAPTER 5: MANAGING STRESS AND ANXIETY

Stress and anxiety are common experiences for students, but they can have a significant impact on academic performance and well-being. In this chapter, we will explore effective strategies to manage stress and anxiety, allowing students to thrive in their academic and personal lives.

The Effects of Stress and Anxiety on Students

Experiencing stress and anxiety can manifest in various ways, including physical symptoms like headaches, fatigue, and difficulty sleeping. Students may also experience emotional symptoms such as irritability, mood swings, and a lack of motivation. The negative effects of stress and anxiety can disrupt concentration, memory, and overall academic performance.

Identifying the Sources of Stress and Anxiety

To effectively manage stress and anxiety, it is essential to identify their sources. Common sources of stress and anxiety for students include academic demands, social pressure, financial concerns, and personal relationships. It may be helpful to keep a journal or make a list of triggers to gain a better understanding of what causes stress and anxiety.

Developing Coping Mechanisms

Once the sources of stress and anxiety have been identified, it is important to develop healthy coping mechanisms to effectively manage them. Some effective strategies include: 1. Time Management: Properly managing time can help reduce stress by creating a sense of control over daily tasks and responsibilities. Prioritize tasks, create a schedule, and break tasks into smaller, manageable steps. 2. Relaxation Techniques: Deep breathing exercises, meditation, and progressive muscle relaxation can help calm the mind and body during times of stress. Engaging in activities such as yoga or taking a walk can also be beneficial in relieving stress. 3. Physical Activity: Regular exercise not only boosts mood and overall well-being but also helps reduce stress and anxiety. Incorporate activities like walking, dancing, or participating in team sports into your routine. 4. Social Support: Seeking support from friends, family, or a support group can provide a sense of connection and perspective. Talking about your feelings and concerns with someone you trust can help alleviate stress and anxiety. 5. Self-Care: Taking care of your physical and emotional needs is crucial for managing stress. Make sure to get enough sleep, eat a balanced diet, engage in activities you enjoy, and prioritize self-care practices like mindfulness or a hobby. 6. Positive Self-Talk: Pay attention to your inner dialogue and challenge negative thoughts. Replace negative thoughts with positive affirmations and realistic perspectives to reduce stress and increase resilience.

Seeking Professional Help

If stress and anxiety become overwhelming and impact your ability to function or enjoy life, it is important to seek professional help. School counselors, therapists, or psychologists can provide guidance and support in managing stress and anxiety. They can also help develop personalized strategies tailored to your specific needs.

Conclusion

Managing stress and anxiety is essential for students to thrive academically and personally. By identifying the sources of stress, developing healthy coping mechanisms, and seeking support when necessary, students can effectively navigate the challenges they face and maintain their well-being. Remember, stress is a natural part of life, but with the right strategies, it can be managed successfully.

Chapter 6: The Importance of Self-Care

In today's fast-paced world, students often find themselves overwhelmed with academic and personal responsibilities. It's easy to get caught up in the hustle and bustle of school life, but it's crucial for students to prioritize their well-being and practice self-care. Taking care of oneself not only promotes good physical and mental health but also enhances academic performance and overall happiness.

THE NEED FOR SELF-CARE

Many students neglect self-care, believing that their focus should solely be on their studies. However, failing to take care of oneself can lead to burnout, high stress levels, and reduced productivity. It's important to remember that self-care is not selfish but rather a necessary component of maintaining balance and personal well-being.

PHYSICAL SELF-CARE

Physical self-care involves taking care of your body through healthy habits. Eating a balanced diet, getting regular exercise, and getting enough sleep are all vital to maintaining good physical health. It's essential to prioritize these activities and make time for them in your daily routine. Engaging in physical activities you enjoy, such as sports or yoga, can also help reduce stress and improve your overall well-being.

MENTAL AND EMOTIONAL SELF-CARE

Caring for your mental and emotional well-being is just as crucial as caring for your physical health. Take time to engage in activities that bring you joy and help you relax, such as reading a book, practicing mindfulness or meditation, or pursuing hobbies and interests outside of academia. It's important to carve out time in your schedule for self-reflection and self-expression.

SOCIAL SELF-CARE

Building and maintaining healthy relationships is an essential aspect of self-care. Surrounding yourself with positive and supportive individuals can significantly impact your well-being. Make time for your friends and loved ones, engage in meaningful conversations, and seek support when needed. Remember to also set boundaries and prioritize your own needs in relationships.

PRACTICAL SELF-CARE STRATEGIES

Here are some practical self-care strategies that you can incorporate into your daily routine:

1. Prioritize self-care activities:

Make self-care activities a non-negotiable part of your schedule. Set dedicated time each day for activities that promote well-being, such as taking a walk, listening to music, or practicing self-reflection.

2. Practice stress management:

Develop healthy coping mechanisms for managing stress, such as deep breathing exercises, journaling, or engaging in relaxation techniques. Find what works best for you and make it a part of your daily routine.

3. Set boundaries:

Learn to say no to activities or commitments that may drain your energy or cause unnecessary stress. Setting boundaries allows you to prioritize your well-being and focus on what truly matters to you.

4. Disconnect from technology:

Give yourself a break from technology and social media. Set aside designated periods without screens to reconnect with yourself and engage in activities that bring you joy.

5. Seek support:

Don't hesitate to reach out for support when needed. Talk to a trusted friend, family member, or counselor about any challenges you may be facing. Remember, seeking help is a sign of strength, not weakness.

INCORPORATING SELF-CARE INTO YOUR LIFE

Self-care should not be seen as a luxury but as an essential part of your daily life. By prioritizing self-care, you will have more energy, focus, and motivation to excel both academically and personally. Remember that self-care is an ongoing practice, and it requires consistent effort and commitment. Embrace the concept of self-care and make it a priority in your life. You deserve it!

Chapter 7: Developing Healthy Habits for Academic Success

Developing healthy habits is essential for students to achieve academic success. By implementing routines and behaviors that support their well-being, students can optimize their learning potential and improve their overall performance. This chapter will explore the importance of developing healthy habits and provide practical strategies for students to incorporate into their daily lives.

THE BENEFITS OF HEALTHY HABITS

Developing healthy habits comes with a wide range of benefits for students. When students prioritize their well-being, they can experience improved focus, increased energy levels, enhanced memory retention, and better overall cognitive function. By implementing healthy habits, students also reduce the risk of burnout, stress, and mental health issues.

Creating a Structured Study Routine

One of the most effective ways to develop healthy habits for academic success is by creating a structured study routine. Establishing a consistent study schedule helps students stay organized, manage their time effectively, and maintain motivation. Designate specific time slots for studying each day and create a productive environment free from distractions.

Getting Sufficient Sleep

Sleep plays a vital role in cognitive function and academic performance. To maximize their learning potential, students should prioritize getting enough sleep each night. Aim for seven to eight hours of uninterrupted sleep to ensure optimal rest and rejuvenation. Develop a relaxing bedtime routine to help transition into a peaceful sleep.

Maintaining a Balanced Diet

A well-balanced diet is crucial for maintaining physical and mental well-being. Students should aim to consume a variety of nutritious foods that provide them with the necessary energy and nutrients for proper brain function. Incorporate fruits, vegetables, whole grains, lean proteins, and healthy fats into your meals to support optimal cognitive performance.

Engaging in Regular Physical Activity

Regular physical activity not only improves physical health but also enhances cognitive abilities. Engaging in exercise boosts blood flow to the brain, promotes the release of mood-enhancing endorphins, and improves focus and concentration. Find activities that you enjoy, such as dancing, swimming, or playing a team sport, and make time for regular exercise.

Staying Hydrated

Proper hydration is often overlooked but is essential for optimal brain function. Dehydration can lead to fatigue, poor concentration, and decreased cognitive performance. Make it a habit to drink an adequate amount of water throughout the day, aiming for at least eight glasses or more, depending on your body's needs.

Taking Regular Breaks

While studying is important, taking regular breaks is equally vital for productivity and well-being. Research suggests that short breaks during study sessions can enhance focus, retention, and overall productivity. Divide your study time into manageable chunks, such as 25-30 minutes of focused studying followed by a 5-10 minute break.

Seeking Social Support

Building a strong support system is essential for maintaining overall well-being. Surround yourself with friends, family, and mentors who encourage and support your academic goals. Engage in meaningful social interactions, collaborative study groups, and seek assistance when needed. Having a support network helps alleviate stress and fosters a positive learning environment.

Implementing Stress Management Techniques

Stress is inevitable, especially for students juggling multiple responsibilities. Implementing stress management techniques can help students cope effectively. Some strategies include deep breathing exercises, mindfulness meditation, journaling, and engaging in hobbies or activities that promote relaxation. Developing healthy habits is crucial for students to thrive academically. By incorporating structured study routines, prioritizing sleep, maintaining a balanced diet, engaging in physical activity, staying hydrated, taking regular breaks, seeking social support, and implementing stress management techniques, students can optimize their well-being and achieve academic success.

Chapter 8: Enhancing Focus and Concentration

In today's fast-paced world filled with distractions, it can be challenging for students to maintain focus and concentration. However, developing the ability to concentrate is crucial for academic success. This chapter will explore strategies to enhance focus and concentration, allowing students to maximize their learning potential.

THE POWER OF MINDFULNESS

One effective technique for enhancing focus and concentration is through the practice of mindfulness. Mindfulness involves intentionally directing one's attention to the present moment, without judgment. By training the mind to stay in the present, students can reduce distractions and improve concentration. Here are a few mindfulness exercises that students can incorporate into their daily routine:

Mindful Breathing:

Take a few moments to focus on your breath. Pay attention to the sensation of each inhale and exhale. Whenever your mind wanders, gently bring your attention back to your breath. This exercise can help anchor your mind in the present moment and improve concentration.

Body Scan:

Find a quiet and comfortable space. Close your eyes and bring your attention to different parts of your body, starting from the top of your head to the tips of your toes. Notice any sensations or areas of tension. This exercise can help relax the body and promote focused attention.

Walking Meditation:

Instead of rushing from one place to another, take a mindful walk. Pay attention to each step, the sensation of your feet touching the ground, and the movements of your body. Engaging your senses in this way can help improve focus and concentration.

CREATING A DISTRACTION-FREE ENVIRONMENT

Another important aspect of enhancing focus and concentration is creating an environment that minimizes distractions. Here are some strategies to create a distraction-free study space:

Remove Electronic Distractions:

Turn off or put away electronic devices such as smartphones, tablets, and laptops, as they can easily divert your attention. Consider using apps or browser extensions that block distracting websites or limit your usage during study sessions.

Organize Your Study Space:

Ensure that your study area is clean, clutter-free, and well-organized. A tidy space can help reduce mental clutter and improve focus. Have all the necessary materials within reach, such as textbooks, notebooks, and stationary.

Manage Noise:

While some students prefer complete silence, others find background noise helpful for concentration. Experiment with different environments to determine what works best for you. You may find ambient sounds, instrumental music, or white noise generators beneficial for focus.

UTILIZING PRODUCTIVITY TECHNIQUES

In addition to mindfulness and creating a distraction-free environment, there are various productivity techniques that can enhance focus and concentration. Here are some popular techniques:

Pomodoro Technique:

The Pomodoro Technique involves working in focused 25-minute intervals, followed by a short break of 5 minutes. After completing four cycles, take a more extended break of 15-30 minutes. This method can help maintain motivation and prevent burnout.

Time Blocking:

Time blocking is the process of scheduling specific blocks of time for different tasks or activities. By assigning dedicated time slots for studying, students can avoid distractions and improve focus. It helps create a sense of structure and prioritize tasks effectively.

Visualizing Success:

Visualizing success involves mentally rehearsing and imagining yourself successfully accomplishing your goals. By visualizing the desired outcome, students can improve focus and motivation. This technique can help maintain concentration during challenging tasks.

CONCLUSION

Enhancing focus and concentration is vital for students to excel academically. By incorporating mindfulness practices, creating a distraction-free environment, and utilizing productivity techniques, students can improve their ability to concentrate and optimize their learning experience. With focused attention, students can achieve their goals and succeed in their academic endeavors.

Chapter 9: Effective Time Management Strategies

Time management is an essential skill for students to master. Without proper time management, it is easy for tasks and responsibilities to pile up, leading to stress and a loss of productivity. In this chapter, we will explore effective strategies that can help students effectively manage their time and achieve their goals.

THE IMPORTANCE OF TIME MANAGEMENT

Time management is crucial for students as it allows them to prioritize tasks, allocate sufficient time to each task, and maintain a healthy work-life balance. By effectively managing their time, students can reduce stress, enhance productivity, and optimize their overall performance.

ANALYZE AND PRIORITIZE TASKS

One of the first steps in effective time management is analyzing and prioritizing tasks. Start by creating a to-do list or using a planner to write down all the tasks and assignments that need to be completed. Once you have a clear picture of what needs to be done, prioritize the tasks based on their deadlines and importance. Focus on completing high-priority tasks first to ensure they are not left until the last minute.

SET REALISTIC GOALS AND DEADLINES

Setting realistic goals and deadlines is essential in time management. Be mindful of your capabilities and the time required to complete each task. Avoid overcommitting yourself and setting unrealistic expectations. Break down larger tasks into smaller, manageable steps, and assign specific deadlines to each step. This will help you stay organized and motivated.

CREATE A SCHEDULE

Creating a schedule is an effective way to manage your time. Allocate specific time slots for different tasks, including studying, attending classes, social activities, and personal time. Be sure to include breaks to rest and recharge. Stick to your schedule as much as possible, but also be flexible to accommodate unexpected events or changes in priorities.

AVOID PROCRASTINATION

Procrastination is the enemy of effective time management. It is important to recognize the signs of procrastination and develop strategies to overcome it. Break tasks into smaller, manageable chunks and focus on completing one chunk at a time. Use techniques such as the Pomodoro

Technique, where you work for a set amount of time (e.g., 25 minutes) and then take a short break (e.g., 5 minutes). This helps maintain focus and prevents burnout.

MINIMIZE DISTRACTIONS

Distractions can significantly hinder your ability to manage your time effectively. Identify potential distractions in your environment, such as social media, noisy surroundings, or unnecessary notifications, and take steps to minimize them. Create a dedicated study space that is free from distractions and turn off notifications on your electronic devices during study sessions.

LEARN TO SAY NO

Part of effective time management is learning to say no to activities or commitments that will overburden your schedule. While it is important to be involved in extracurricular activities and social events, it is equally important to prioritize your academic responsibilities. Be selective in how you spend your time and learn to prioritize tasks that align with your goals and values.

SEEK SUPPORT AND ACCOUNTABILITY

Managing time effectively can be challenging, especially when faced with competing priorities. It can be helpful to seek support from peers, family members, or mentors who can provide guidance and accountability. Share your goals and deadlines with them, and ask for their assistance in staying on track.

REFLECT AND ADAPT

Regularly reflecting on your time management practices and making necessary adjustments is crucial for long-term success. Assess what strategies are working well and identify areas for improvement. Be willing to adapt and try different techniques to find what works best for you. In conclusion, effective time management is essential for students to achieve academic success and maintain a healthy work-life balance. By analyzing and prioritizing tasks, setting realistic goals and deadlines, creating a schedule, avoiding procrastination, minimizing distractions, learning to say no, seeking support and accountability, and reflecting and adapting, students can develop strong time management skills that will benefit them both academically and personally.

Chapter 10: Overcoming Procrastination

Procrastination is a common challenge that many students face. It can prevent you from reaching your full potential and can lead to increased stress and anxiety. In this chapter, we will explore strategies to help you overcome procrastination and develop productive study habits.

THE CAUSES OF PROCRASTINATION

Procrastination can have various causes, and it is essential to understand them to effectively address this issue. Some common causes of procrastination include:

1. Fear of Failure:

Some students may postpone starting a task because they fear that they will not meet their own expectations or receive criticism from others. The fear of failure can be paralyzing, leading to avoidance and procrastination.

2. Lack of Motivation:

When you lack interest or motivation in a particular task, it is easy to delay starting or completing it. This lack of motivation can stem from various factors such as a lack of understanding of the task's relevance, low self-efficacy, or a feeling of overwhelm.

3. Perfectionism:

Students who have perfectionistic tendencies may put off starting a task because they are always seeking perfection. They have an underlying belief that if they cannot complete a task perfectly, there is no point in doing it at all.

4. Poor Time Management:

Inadequate time management skills can lead to procrastination. If you fail to prioritize tasks effectively or underestimate the time required to complete them, you may find yourself constantly leaving things until the last minute.

STRATEGIES TO OVERCOME PROCRASTINATION

Now that we have identified some common causes of procrastination let's explore strategies to overcome this habit and become more productive.

1. Break Tasks into Smaller Steps:

When faced with a large and overwhelming task, it is easy to procrastinate. Break the task down into smaller, more manageable steps. This will make the task appear less daunting and help you get started.

2. Set Clear Goals and Deadlines:

Set specific and realistic goals for each task. Establish deadlines for completing these goals to create a sense of urgency and accountability. Having clear objectives and timelines will motivate you to start working on the task promptly.

3. Use the Pomodoro Technique:

The Pomodoro Technique is a time management method that involves working in focused bursts followed by short breaks. Set a timer for 25 minutes, work on the task with full concentration during this time, and then take a 5-minute break. Repeat this cycle several times, and then reward yourself with a more extended break. This technique helps to combat procrastination by breaking tasks into manageable intervals and maintaining focus.

4. Minimize Distractions:

Identify and minimize distractions in your environment. Put away your phone, close unnecessary tabs on your computer, and create a dedicated study space that is free from distractions. By eliminating potential disturbances, you can maintain focus and resist the temptation to procrastinate.

5. Utilize Productivity Apps and Tools:

There are several productivity apps and tools available that can help you stay organized and focused. Consider using apps that allow you to create to-do lists, set reminders, and track your progress. These tools can help you stay on track and hold yourself accountable.

6. Practice Self-Compassion:

Be kind and understanding towards yourself when you find yourself procrastinating. Remember that everyone struggles with procrastination at times, and it does not define your worth as a student. Practice self-compassion and give yourself permission to make mistakes and learn from them. By implementing these strategies, you can overcome procrastination and develop productive study habits. Remember, change takes time and effort, so be patient with yourself as you work towards breaking the habit of procrastination. Start small, celebrate your progress, and keep pushing forward. You have the power to overcome procrastination and achieve academic success.Improving Study Skills

STRATEGIES FOR EFFECTIVE STUDYING

Developing strong study skills is essential for academic success. In this chapter, we will explore various strategies to help students improve their study habits and maximize their learning potential.

1. Create a Study Schedule

One of the first steps in improving study skills is creating a study schedule. By allocating dedicated time for studying each day, you can establish a routine and ensure that you have enough time to cover all the necessary material. Consider your own peak cognitive hours and try to schedule your most challenging subjects during that time.

2. Find a Quiet and Distraction-Free Environment

Your study environment plays a significant role in your concentration and focus. Find a quiet place where you can minimize distractions to optimize your productivity. Turn off your phone or put it on silent mode, and avoid studying in places where you are likely to be interrupted.

3. Utilize Active Learning Techniques

Passively reading textbooks or notes is not an effective way of studying. Instead, engage in active learning techniques that encourage critical thinking and deep understanding. Some examples include: - Taking handwritten notes: Writing notes helps you process information and reinforce your understanding of the material. - Summarizing and paraphrasing: Practice summarizing complex concepts or passages in your own words to enhance comprehension. - Participating in group discussions: Explaining concepts to others and engaging in discussions can deepen your understanding and provide different perspectives.

4. Use Visualization and Mind Mapping

Visualization and mind mapping are powerful tools for improving memory and understanding complex topics. Create visual representations of the information you are studying, whether through diagrams, charts, or mind maps. These visual aids can help you organize and connect ideas, making it easier to recall and understand the material.

5. Take Regular Breaks

Studying for hours without breaks can lead to burnout and reduced focus. Instead, adopt the Pomodoro Technique, which involves studying for a focused 25-minute session followed by a short 5-minute break. After completing four Pomodoro cycles, take a longer break of around 15-30 minutes. This method allows for regular rest intervals, improving concentration and overall productivity.

6. Practice Retrieval and Spaced Repetition

Retrieval practice is the act of recalling information from memory, and it has been proven to be an effective study technique. Instead of simply rereading your materials, actively test yourself by trying to recall key concepts or answering practice questions. Spaced repetition involves reviewing information at gradually increasing intervals, which helps reinforce long-term memory.

7. Seek Clarification and Ask Questions

Don't hesitate to seek clarification or ask questions when you encounter difficulties. Consulting with your teachers, classmates, or tutors can provide clarification and deepen your understanding. Active engagement with the material and seeking clarification when needed can significantly enhance your overall study experience.

8. Practice Self-Care

Lastly, remember to take care of yourself while studying. Ensure you are getting enough sleep, eating nutritious meals, and engaging in physical activity. Taking care of your physical and mental well-being is crucial for optimal cognitive functioning and improved study skills. By implementing these strategies, you can enhance your study skills and make the most of your study time. Remember, effective studying is not just about putting in hours but also adopting the right techniques and creating a conducive learning environment. Develop a growth mindset, stay motivated, and embrace the journey of continuous learning. Happy studying! Next up, Chapter 12: Effective Note-Taking Techniques.

Chapter 12: Effective Note-Taking Techniques

Taking effective notes is a critical skill that can greatly enhance your learning and understanding of the material. In this chapter, we will explore various techniques and strategies to help you become a more proficient note-taker.

THE IMPORTANCE OF NOTE-TAKING

Note-taking is not merely the act of transcribing information from a lecture or reading. It is an active process that promotes engagement, organization, and retention of information. Here are some key reasons why effective note-taking is essential:

1. Enhances Learning

Taking well-structured and concise notes allows you to actively process and summarize the information. This engagement helps you understand and internalize the material more effectively than passive listening or reading alone.

2. Facilitates Review and Recall

Revisiting your notes later helps reinforce your understanding and aids in long-term retention. Well-organized and clear notes make it easier to review and recall important points when studying for exams or writing assignments.

3. Provides a Personal Reference

Your notes serve as a personal reference that captures key ideas, concepts, examples, and explanations. They can provide valuable information when reviewing for future courses or when looking back on your academic journey.

EFFECTIVE NOTE-TAKING STRATEGIES

Now let's dive into some practical strategies you can employ to optimize your note-taking skills:

1. Be Selective

Instead of trying to write down every word, focus on capturing the main ideas, key concepts, and supporting details. This allows you to actively listen and engage with the material rather than becoming overwhelmed with transcribing everything.

2. Use Abbreviations and Symbols

Develop your own system of abbreviations and symbols to save time and space while taking notes. For example, using an arrow to represent "leads to," or using the symbol "&" instead of writing "and."

3. Organize Your Notes

Create a clear and organized structure for your notes. Use headings, bullet points, numbering, and indentation to differentiate main ideas from supporting details. Color coding or highlighting can also be helpful in visually categorizing information.

4. Utilize Visual Aids

Drawing diagrams, charts, and graphs can visually represent complex concepts and enhance understanding. Visual aids can also serve as valuable memory prompts when reviewing your notes.

5. Leave Space for Elaboration

Leave extra space between points to add additional comments, questions, or reflections later on. This allows you to expand on ideas during review sessions or when discussing the material with classmates or instructors.

6. Review and Revise Regularly

Set aside dedicated time to review and revise your notes regularly. Consolidate information, clarify any misunderstandings, and fill in any gaps. Actively engaging with your notes improves retention and supports deeper learning.

7. Use Technology Appropriately

Digital tools like note-taking apps, tablets, and laptops can be useful for organizing and accessing notes. However, be mindful of potential distractions and remember that handwritten notes have been shown to enhance learning and retention.

CONCLUSION

Mastering effective note-taking techniques is a valuable skill that can significantly contribute to your academic success. By being selective, organized, and engaged in the note-taking process, you can enhance your learning, improve your recall, and ultimately thrive in your academic pursuits. Remember, the goal of note-taking is not simply to transcribe information but to actively engage with the material, make connections, and create a personal reference that supports your learning journey. So, apply these strategies and find a note-taking approach that works best for you. Happy note-taking! Boosting Memory and Retention Memory and retention are essential skills for students to succeed academically. Being able to remember and retain information not only helps in exams and assignments but also in building a strong foundation of knowledge. In this chapter, we will explore effective strategies to boost memory and retention, allowing students to retain information for the long term and apply it when needed.

UNDERSTANDING HOW MEMORY WORKS

Before we dive into specific techniques, it's important to have a basic understanding of how memory works. Our memory is divided into three stages: encoding, storage, and retrieval. During the encoding stage, information is initially processed and encoded into our memory. The storage stage involves the retention of information over time, and retrieval refers to the ability to recall and access stored information.

UTILIZING EFFECTIVE STUDY TECHNIQUES

One of the most effective study techniques for boosting memory and retention is active learning. Instead of passively reading or listening to information, actively engage with the material. Some strategies to incorporate active learning include:

1. Spaced Repetition

Spacing out your study sessions over time is more effective for long-term retention compared to cramming. Reviewing information at spaced intervals allows your brain to strengthen the connections between neurons, making it easier to recall the information later on.

2. Mnemonic Devices

Mnemonic devices are memory aids that help you remember information by associating it with something more memorable. This could be creating acronyms, rhymes, or visual associations. For example, to remember the order of the planets in our solar system, you can use the phrase "My Very Eager Mother Just Served Us Nachos" (Mercury, Venus, Earth, Mars, Jupiter, Saturn, Uranus, Neptune).

3. Visualization and Mind Mapping

Visualizing concepts and creating mind maps can enhance memory retention. Picture the information in your mind or create diagrams and flowcharts that connect related concepts. This visual representation helps your brain organize and recall information more effectively.

4. Retrieval Practice

Instead of simply reviewing your notes or textbooks, actively test yourself on the material. Practice recalling information without referring to external sources. This act of retrieval strengthens memory pathways and helps you remember the information more easily in the future.

5. Teach or Explain the Material

One of the most effective ways to solidify your learning is by teaching or explaining the material to someone else. This forces you to break down complex ideas into simpler terms and helps reinforce your understanding of the subject matter.

CREATING A SUPPORTIVE ENVIRONMENT

Apart from utilizing effective study techniques, creating a supportive environment can also boost memory and retention. Here are some tips to consider:

1. Minimize Distractions

Find a quiet and dedicated study space free from distractions. Turn off notifications on your phone and computer, and create a conducive environment that allows you to focus solely on your studies.

2. Get Sufficient Sleep

Adequate sleep is crucial for memory consolidation. Make sure you get enough restful sleep each night to allow your brain to process and retain information effectively.

3. Stay Physically Active

Regular physical activity has been shown to improve memory and cognitive function. Incorporate exercise into your daily routine to reap the benefits of an active lifestyle.

4. Practice Mindfulness and Relaxation Techniques

Stress and anxiety can hinder memory and retention. Practice mindfulness and relaxation techniques such as deep breathing, meditation, or yoga to reduce stress levels and improve focus.

CONCLUSION

Boosting memory and retention is essential for students to succeed in their academic endeavors. By utilizing effective study techniques, creating a supportive environment, and practicing consistent habits, students can enhance their ability to retain information and apply it when needed. Remember, memory is a skill that can be developed and improved with practice, so don't be discouraged if you face challenges initially. Keep implementing these strategies, and you will see a significant improvement in your memory and retention abilities.

Chapter 14: Increasing Productivity

In today's fast-paced world, students are often faced with numerous distractions that can hinder their productivity. However, by implementing effective strategies and techniques, students can increase their productivity and make the most of their study time. This chapter explores various methods to help students stay focused, manage their time effectively, and accomplish tasks efficiently.

CREATING A PRODUCTIVE ENVIRONMENT

One of the first steps in increasing productivity is to create a conducive environment for studying. Here are some tips to help you create a productive workspace:

Minimize Distractions

Eliminate or minimize distractions that can divert your attention away from your work. This includes turning off notifications on your phone, closing unnecessary tabs on your computer, and finding a quiet location where you can concentrate without interruptions.

Organize Your Workspace

A cluttered workspace can be a visual distraction and may hinder your ability to focus. Take some time to declutter and organize your study area. Keep essential materials within reach and ensure that your workspace is clean and well-lit.

Utilize Productivity Tools

There are numerous productivity tools available that can help you stay organized and manage your tasks efficiently. Consider using apps or software that enable you to create to-do lists, set reminders, and track your progress. Some popular productivity tools include Todoist, Trello, and Evernote.

EFFECTIVE TIME MANAGEMENT TECHNIQUES

Time management plays a vital role in increasing productivity. By utilizing effective time management techniques, students can allocate their time wisely and complete tasks more efficiently. Here are some techniques to help you manage your time effectively:

Set Priorities

Identify and prioritize your most important tasks. By focusing on the tasks that are most crucial, you can ensure that your time is used efficiently. Consider using the Eisenhower Matrix, a popular method for prioritizing tasks based on their urgency and importance.

Use Time Blocking

Time blocking involves scheduling specific blocks of time for different activities. Create a daily or weekly schedule that includes dedicated study time, breaks, and other commitments. This helps provide structure to your day and ensures that you allocate enough time for each task.

Practice the Pomodoro Technique

The Pomodoro Technique is a time management method that involves working in focused bursts, known as Pomodoros, followed by short breaks. Set a timer for a specific period, such as 25 minutes, and work on a task until the timer goes off. Then, take a short break before starting the next Pomodoro. This technique helps improve focus and productivity by breaking tasks into manageable chunks.

IMPLEMENTING EFFECTIVE TASK MANAGEMENT STRATEGIES

In addition to time management, effectively managing your tasks can greatly increase productivity. Here are some strategies to help you manage your tasks more efficiently:

Break Tasks into Smaller Steps

Large tasks can be overwhelming, which can lead to procrastination. Break down your tasks into smaller, more manageable steps. This not only makes the tasks less intimidating but also allows you to make progress incrementally.

Utilize a Planner or Task Management System

A planner or a task management system can help you keep track of your assignments, deadlines, and progress on different tasks. Find a system that works for you, whether it's a physical planner, a digital calendar, or a task management app. Make sure to regularly update and review your planner to stay organized and on top of your tasks.

Practice the Two-Minute Rule

The Two-Minute Rule states that if a task takes less than two minutes to complete, you should do it immediately rather than postponing it. This rule helps prevent small tasks from accumulating and becoming overwhelming. By quickly completing these small tasks, you free up mental energy and focus on more significant tasks. By implementing these strategies and techniques, you can increase your productivity and make the most of your study time. Remember that everyone's productivity methods may vary, so experiment with different techniques to find what works best for you. Stay disciplined, stay focused, and you'll be amazed at how much you can accomplish.

Chapter 15: Managing Distractions in the Digital Age

In today's digital age, students are heavily exposed to a wide array of distractions that can hinder their focus and productivity. With constant access to social media, online games, and other forms of entertainment, it has become increasingly challenging to stay focused on academic tasks. However, by adopting effective strategies, students can learn to manage these distractions and make the most of their study time.

UNDERSTANDING THE IMPACT OF DIGITAL DISTRACTIONS

The first step in managing distractions is to recognize their impact on academic performance. When students constantly switch their attention between studying and checking their phones or engaging in online activities, their ability to concentrate and retain information significantly decreases. These distractions can lead to decreased productivity, increased time spent on tasks, and ultimately, lower grades.

CREATING A DISTRACTION-FREE ENVIRONMENT

One effective strategy for managing distractions is to create a dedicated study environment that minimizes the presence of digital temptations. This means finding a quiet space away from electronic devices, such as turning off notifications or using apps that limit access to certain websites or apps during study sessions. By creating a distraction-free zone, students can better focus on their work and avoid the constant pull of digital distractions.

IMPLEMENTING THE POMODORO TECHNIQUE

The Pomodoro Technique is a time management strategy that can help students effectively manage their study time while minimizing distractions. The technique involves breaking study sessions into short intervals, typically 25 minutes, followed by a short break of 5 minutes. After completing four consecutive intervals, students can take a longer break of 15 to 30 minutes. This technique not only encourages focused work but also allows students to acknowledge and indulge in distractions during the predetermined breaks.

UTILIZING PRODUCTIVITY APPS AND TOOLS

In addition to creating a distraction-free environment and using time management techniques, students can also leverage various productivity apps and tools to help them stay focused. There are apps available that can block specific websites and apps during study sessions, track and analyze time usage, set reminders and deadlines, and even provide motivational messages to keep students on track.

PRACTICING MINDFULNESS AND SELF-DISCIPLINE

Mindfulness and self-discipline are powerful tools for managing distractions. By practicing mindfulness, students can train their minds to stay present and focused on their tasks, reducing the tendency to get derailed by digital temptations. Additionally, cultivating self-discipline allows students to resist the immediate gratification of digital distractions and prioritize their long-term goals and academic success.

SEEKING ACCOUNTABILITY AND SUPPORT

Sometimes, managing distractions requires external support and accountability. Students can benefit from studying with a partner or forming study groups where they can hold each other accountable and provide a distraction-free environment. Additionally, seeking guidance from teachers or academic advisors can help students develop effective strategies for managing distractions specific to their individual needs. Managing distractions in the digital age is not an easy task, but with the right strategies and mindset, students can regain control over their attention and focus. By creating a distraction-free environment, implementing time management techniques, utilizing productivity apps, practicing mindfulness and self-discipline, and seeking support when needed, students can optimize their study time and achieve greater academic success.

Chapter 16: Effective Communication Skills

Good communication skills are essential for students to succeed academically and personally. Effective communication allows students to express their ideas, collaborate with others, and build positive relationships. In this chapter, we will explore various strategies and techniques to improve communication skills in different contexts.

1. ACTIVE LISTENING

One of the most important aspects of effective communication is active listening.

Active listening involves paying attention to the speaker, understanding their message, and responding appropriately. To become a better listener, students can: - Maintain eye contact and provide verbal and nonverbal cues to show that they are engaged. - Avoid interrupting or finishing the speaker's sentences. - Ask clarifying questions to ensure understanding. - Paraphrase the speaker's message to demonstrate comprehension. - Avoid distractions and give full attention to the speaker. By practicing active listening, students can enhance their understanding of others' perspectives and improve the quality of their interactions.

2. VERBAL COMMUNICATION

Verbal communication involves the use of words to convey messages and ideas. Effective verbal communication requires clarity, conciseness, and appropriate language. Here are some tips for improving verbal communication skills: - Speak clearly and audibly, adjusting the volume and tone of your voice to suit the situation. - Use appropriate language and tone for the audience and context. - Organize your thoughts before speaking to ensure coherence and clarity. - Avoid using jargon or technical terms that may confuse others. - Be mindful of nonverbal cues such as facial expressions, gestures, and body language to enhance your message. Practicing effective verbal communication will enable students to express their thoughts and ideas clearly, leading to better understanding and engagement with peers, teachers, and other individuals they interact with.

3. WRITTEN COMMUNICATION

Written communication plays a significant role in academic settings. Whether it's writing essays, reports, or emails, students need to convey their thoughts effectively through writing. Here are some strategies to improve written communication skills: - Organize your thoughts before writing, outlining main points and supporting details. - Use clear and concise language, avoiding unnecessary jargon or complex terms. - Proofread and edit your writing for grammar, spelling, and punctuation errors. - Use appropriate formatting and structure for different types of written communication. - Seek feedback from teachers, peers, or writing centers to enhance your writing skills. By honing their written communication skills, students can effectively convey their ideas, showcase their knowledge, and present their work in a professional manner.

4. NONVERBAL COMMUNICATION

Nonverbal communication includes body language, facial expressions, gestures, and tone of voice. These nonverbal cues can convey messages or emotions without the use of words. Here are some tips for improving nonverbal communication: - Maintain appropriate eye contact to demonstrate attentiveness and interest. - Use facial expressions and gestures that align with your intended message. - Be aware of your tone of voice and ensure it communicates the intended emotions. - Pay attention to others' nonverbal cues to gauge their reactions and adjust your communication accordingly. Being mindful of nonverbal cues and using them effectively can enhance the clarity and impact of your communication.

5. CONFLICT RESOLUTION

Effective communication skills also play a vital role in resolving conflicts and disagreements. When faced with conflicts, students can use the following strategies: - Actively listen to understand the perspectives and concerns of all parties involved. - Use "I" statements to express thoughts and feelings without blaming others. - Seek common ground and focus on shared goals or interests. - Use respectful and constructive language to communicate assertively. - Collaborate with others to find mutually beneficial solutions. By practicing effective communication skills, students can navigate conflicts more effectively, build stronger relationships, and create a positive and supportive learning environment.

CONCLUSION

Effective communication skills are essential for students to thrive in academic and personal life. By practicing active listening, improving verbal and written communication, being mindful of nonverbal cues, and developing conflict resolution skills, students can enhance their communication abilities. These skills will not only benefit them academically but also in their future careers and personal relationships.

CHAPTER 17: BUILDING POSITIVE RELATIONSHIPS

Building positive relationships is essential for students to thrive in both their academic and personal lives. Having a strong support system of friends, mentors, and peers can provide encouragement, motivation, and a sense of belonging. In this chapter, we will explore strategies and tips for building positive relationships that contribute to overall happiness and success.

1. Foster open and effective communication:

Communication is key in any relationship. It is important to express your thoughts, feelings, and needs in a clear and respectful manner. Additionally, active listening is crucial to understanding others and building stronger connections. Practice empathy and avoid making assumptions. By being open and honest in your communication, you can establish trust and deepen your relationships.

2. Seek common interests:

One way to build positive relationships is by connecting with others who share similar interests and hobbies. Join clubs or organizations that align with your passions and values. Attend social events or community activities where you can meet people who have similar goals and aspirations. Engaging in shared activities can foster a sense of camaraderie and create lasting bonds.

3. Show appreciation and gratitude:

Expressing gratitude and appreciation is a simple yet powerful way to build positive relationships. Take the time to acknowledge and thank those who have supported you along the way. It can be as simple as sending a thank you note, offering a heartfelt compliment, or publicly recognizing someone's efforts. By showing gratitude, you not only strengthen your relationships but also foster a positive and supportive environment.

4. Be a good listener:

Being a good listener is vital in building positive relationships. Actively listen to others without interrupting or judging. Show genuine interest in what others have to say by asking questions and providing affirmation. This demonstrates respect and validates the other person's feelings and experiences.

5. Practice empathy and understanding:

Empathy is the ability to understand and share the feelings of others. By practicing empathy, you can deepen your connections with others. Put yourself in someone else's shoes and try to see things from their perspective. This will help you build trust, resolve conflicts, and develop more meaningful relationships.

6. Be supportive and offer help:

Being supportive and offering help when needed can strengthen relationships. Be there for your friends, classmates, and colleagues when they face challenges or need assistance. Celebrate their accomplishments and provide encouragement during difficult times. Being a reliable and supportive presence fosters a sense of trust and deepens connections.

7. Resolve conflicts in a healthy manner:

Conflicts are a natural part of any relationship. However, it is important to address conflicts in a healthy and respectful manner. Communicate your concerns calmly and listen to the other person's perspective. Find a compromise that is mutually beneficial. Resolving conflicts in a healthy manner can strengthen relationships and improve overall communication.

8. Surround yourself with positive influences:

Choose to surround yourself with people who uplift and inspire you. Avoid toxic or negative individuals who drain your energy and hinder your growth. Seek out positive role models, mentors, and friends who support your goals and aspirations. Surrounding yourself with positive influences can have a significant impact on your overall well-being and success.

Conclusion:

Building positive relationships is an important aspect of the happiness mindset for students. By fostering open communication, seeking common interests, showing appreciation, practicing empathy, offering support, resolving conflicts in a healthy manner, and surrounding yourself with positive influences, you can cultivate meaningful and supportive relationships that contribute to your overall happiness and success. Remember, relationships take time and effort to develop, so be patient and invest in building connections that will enrich your life.

Chapter 18: Coping with Academic Pressure

Academic pressure is something that most students face at some point in their educational journey. The demands of school work, exams, deadlines, and high expectations can create a significant amount of stress and anxiety. In this chapter, we will explore strategies and techniques to cope with academic pressure and maintain a healthy mindset.

RECOGNIZING THE SIGNS OF ACADEMIC PRESSURE

It's important to be able to recognize the signs and symptoms of academic pressure so that we can address it before it becomes overwhelming. Some common signs include:

Physical symptoms:

- Frequent headaches or stomachaches - Sleep disturbances - Loss of appetite or overeating - Fatigue or low energy levels

Emotional symptoms:

- Feeling overwhelmed or constantly worried - Irritability or mood swings - Difficulty concentrating or making decisions - Increased self-criticism or negative self-talk

DEVELOPING HEALTHY COPING MECHANISMS

When faced with academic pressure, it's essential to develop healthy coping mechanisms to manage stress and maintain well-being. Here are some strategies you can try:

1. Practice self-care:

Make sure to prioritize self-care activities such as getting enough sleep, eating a balanced diet, exercising regularly, and engaging in activities you enjoy. Taking care of your physical and mental well-being will provide you with the resilience to handle academic pressure.

2. Seek support:

Reach out to friends, family members, or teachers who can provide support and understanding. Talking about your feelings and concerns can help to alleviate some of the pressure and give you a fresh perspective.

3. Break tasks into smaller steps:

Feeling overwhelmed with a large task or assignment is common when experiencing academic pressure. Break down the task into smaller, more manageable steps. This will help you stay organized and focused.

4. Set realistic goals:

Set realistic and achievable goals for yourself. Break your larger academic goals into smaller milestones and celebrate your progress along the way. This will help you stay motivated and avoid feeling overwhelmed.

5. Practice time management:

Effective time management can reduce stress and help you stay on top of your academic workload. Prioritize tasks, create a schedule, and allocate specific time slots for studying, completing assignments, and taking breaks.

6. Utilize relaxation techniques:

Incorporate relaxation techniques such as deep breathing exercises, meditation, or mindfulness practices into your daily routine. These techniques can help you relax your body and mind, reducing feelings of stress and anxiety.

7. Challenge negative thoughts:

Be aware of negative thoughts or self-doubt that may arise when facing academic pressure. Challenge these thoughts by reframing them into more positive and realistic perspectives. Focus on your strengths and past successes to boost your confidence.

8. Take breaks:

Don't forget to give yourself regular breaks during your study sessions. Taking short breaks can help you recharge, improve focus, and prevent burnout. Engage in activities that help you relax and clear your mind, such as going for a walk or listening to music.

SEEKING ADDITIONAL SUPPORT

If academic pressure becomes overwhelming and starts impacting your mental health and well-being, it's essential to seek professional support. Reach out to a school counselor, therapist, or mental health professional who can provide guidance and help you develop effective coping strategies. Remember, academic pressure is a temporary challenge that you have the power to overcome. By implementing these coping strategies and seeking support when needed, you can navigate the demands of academia while maintaining your mental and emotional well-being. Next up:

CHAPTER 19: DEVELOPING A HEALTHY WORK-LIFE BALANCE

CHAPTER 19: DEVELOPING A HEALTHY WORK-LIFE BALANCE

In today's fast-paced and demanding world, many students struggle to find a balance between their academic responsibilities and personal life. It can be challenging to juggle coursework, extracurricular activities, part-time jobs, and social commitments, often resulting in stress, burnout, and a lack of overall well-being. However, developing a healthy work-life balance is crucial for maintaining physical and mental health, as well as maximizing academic performance and personal fulfillment. It allows students to engage in their studies effectively while also having time for relaxation, hobbies, and socialization. Here are some practical strategies for developing a healthy work-life balance:

1. Prioritize and Set Boundaries:

Identify your priorities and allocate your time accordingly. Determine the most important tasks and focus on them first. Set boundaries by establishing specific periods for studying, engaging in extracurricular activities, and relaxing. Avoid overcommitting yourself and learn to say no when necessary.

2. Create a Schedule:

Develop a weekly or monthly schedule that includes designated time slots for studying, attending classes, participating in extracurricular activities, and personal time. Adhering to a schedule helps you stay organized and ensures that you allocate sufficient time for both academic and personal pursuits.

3. Practice Effective Time Management:

Learn effective time management techniques, such as prioritizing tasks, breaking them into smaller manageable chunks, and utilizing tools like to-do lists, calendars, and productivity apps. By using these strategies, you can make the most of your time and accomplish tasks efficiently, leaving room for leisure and enjoyment.

4. Engage in Self-Care:

Take care of your physical and mental well-being by prioritizing self-care activities. This may include getting enough sleep, eating nutritious meals, engaging in regular exercise, practicing mindfulness or meditation, and seeking support from friends, family, or mental health professionals when needed. Remember that taking care of yourself is not selfish but essential for sustained success and happiness.

5. Delegate and Seek Support:

It's essential to recognize that you don't have to do everything on your own. Delegate tasks whenever possible, whether it's group work, household chores, or personal responsibilities. Additionally, don't hesitate to seek support from friends, family, or academic resources when you encounter difficulties or feel overwhelmed.

6. Disconnect from Technology:

Constant connectivity through technology can blur the lines between work and personal life. Make a conscious effort to disconnect from emails, social media, and other distractions during designated personal time. This allows you to fully engage in activities outside of academics and establish a healthy separation between different aspects of your life.

7. Set Realistic Expectations:

Avoid setting unrealistic expectations for yourself in terms of academic achievement and extracurricular involvement. Recognize that striving for perfection is not sustainable or necessary. Set realistic goals, evaluate your progress regularly, and adjust your expectations accordingly. Remember, balance and well-being should be your ultimate priorities. Finding a healthy work-life balance is an ongoing process that requires continuous assessment and adjustment. It's important to regularly check in with yourself, evaluate your priorities, and make necessary changes to ensure that you are nurturing both your academic and personal lives. By developing a healthy work-life balance, you can create an environment that supports your overall well-being, enhances your academic success, and brings fulfillment to your personal life. Remember, achieving balance is not about perfect equilibrium but rather finding a harmony that works for you.

Chapter 20: Embracing Failure as a Learning Opportunity

Failure is often seen as a negative and undesirable outcome. In our society, we are conditioned to believe that failure is something to be ashamed of, a sign of incompetence or inadequacy. However, this perspective on failure is limiting and misguided. In reality, failure is a natural part of life and can be a valuable learning opportunity, especially for students. When we embrace failure as a learning opportunity, we shift our mindset and open ourselves up to growth and personal development. Instead of dwelling on our mistakes and feeling discouraged, we can approach failure with curiosity and a desire to improve. By reframing failure in this way, we can cultivate resilience, develop problem-solving skills, and ultimately achieve greater success. One of the first steps in embracing failure as a learning opportunity is to change our perception of failure. Instead of viewing failure as a reflection of our worth or abilities, we can see it as a stepping stone on the path to success. Failure provides valuable feedback and teaches us important lessons about ourselves and the world around us. To effectively embrace failure, it is essential to adopt a growth mindset. A growth mindset is the belief that our abilities and intelligence can be developed through hard work, dedication, and perseverance. With a growth mindset, we understand that failure is not a permanent condition but rather an opportunity for improvement and personal growth. By cultivating a growth mindset, we can overcome setbacks, bounce back from failure, and continue to strive for success. Another important aspect of embracing failure is to practice self-compassion. It is natural to feel disappointed or frustrated when we fail, but it is crucial to treat ourselves with kindness and understanding. Rather than beating ourselves up over our mistakes, we can acknowledge our efforts and recognize that failure is a part of the learning process. By practicing self-compassion, we can learn from our failures and move forward with renewed motivation and resilience. In order to fully embrace failure as a learning opportunity, it is important to reflect on our failures and extract the valuable lessons they offer. This reflection process involves asking ourselves questions such as: What went wrong? What can I learn from this experience? How can I apply these lessons in the future? By actively seeking the lessons within our failures, we can turn them into stepping stones towards success. Lastly, it is important to surround ourselves with a supportive network of peers, mentors, and teachers who encourage and motivate us to embrace failure as a learning opportunity. Having a supportive environment can make a significant difference in how we perceive and respond to failure. When we have people who believe in us and help us see the potential for growth in our failures, we are more likely to embrace failure and use it as a springboard for future success. In conclusion, failure is not something to be feared or avoided but rather embraced as a learning opportunity. By shifting our mindset, practicing self-compassion, adopting a growth mindset, reflecting on our failures, and surrounding ourselves with a supportive network, we can turn failure into a powerful tool for personal and academic growth. So, instead of fearing failure, let us embrace it, learn from it, and use it to propel ourselves towards success.

Chapter 21: Finding Purpose and Meaning in Education

Education is about more than just acquiring knowledge and skills. It is a journey of self-discovery and personal growth. In order to truly thrive in your academic and personal life, it is important to find purpose and meaning in your education.

UNDERSTANDING THE IMPORTANCE OF PURPOSE

Having a sense of purpose in your education can motivate and inspire you to persevere and excel. When you have a clear understanding of why you are pursuing your education, it becomes much easier to navigate through challenges and setbacks. Purpose gives your studies a sense of direction and fulfillment, making your journey more meaningful.

REFLECTING ON YOUR VALUES AND PASSIONS

To find purpose in your education, start by reflecting on your values and passions. Ask yourself: What is important to me? What subjects or topics am I genuinely interested in? What kind of impact do I want to make in the world? Identifying your values and passions will help you align your educational pursuits with your personal goals and aspirations.

SETTING MEANINGFUL GOALS

Once you have a clear understanding of your values and passions, it is essential to set meaningful goals. Goals provide you with a sense of direction and purpose, ensuring that your educational journey is focused and purpose-driven. Whether it is getting accepted into your dream college, pursuing a specific career path, or making a difference in your community, set goals that resonate with your values and passions.

SEEKING OPPORTUNITIES FOR GROWTH AND IMPACT

Finding purpose in education involves seeking opportunities for growth and impact. Look for ways to challenge yourself academically, such as taking advanced courses or participating in research projects. Engage in extracurricular activities that allow you to make a positive difference in your community, such as volunteering or joining clubs and organizations. By actively seeking opportunities for growth and impact, you can cultivate a sense of purpose and meaning in your education.

EMBRACING A GROWTH MINDSET

Adopting a growth mindset is crucial in finding purpose and meaning in education.

Embrace the belief that your abilities and intelligence can be developed through dedication and hard work. See challenges as opportunities for growth and view setbacks as learning experiences. By cultivating a growth mindset, you will approach your education with a sense of curiosity, resilience, and determination, which will ultimately lead to a deeper sense of purpose and fulfillment.

CONNECTING YOUR EDUCATION TO THE BIGGER PICTURE

To find purpose and meaning in education, it is important to connect your studies to the bigger picture. Explore how your education can contribute to the betterment of society or how it aligns with your personal values and long-term goals. By understanding the significance of your education beyond the classroom, you will be able to see the purpose and impact of your studies, making your educational journey all the more meaningful.

PRACTICING GRATITUDE AND APPRECIATION

Finally, practicing gratitude and appreciation can help you find purpose and meaning in education. Take time to reflect on the opportunities and resources available to you, and express gratitude for the teachers, mentors, and peers who have supported you along the way. By acknowledging and appreciating the value of your education, you will develop a deeper sense of purpose and motivation to make the most out of your educational experience. Finding purpose and meaning in education is a lifelong process. It requires self-reflection, goal-setting, embracing challenges, and connecting with the bigger picture. By actively seeking purpose in your education, you will not only thrive academically, but also find fulfillment and satisfaction in your personal and professional life.

Chapter 22: Cultivating Gratitude and Appreciation

In this chapter, we will explore the powerful practice of cultivating gratitude and appreciation in the lives of students. Gratitude is the act of recognizing and acknowledging the good things in our lives, big or small, and appreciating them. When we cultivate gratitude and appreciation, we shift our focus from what is lacking to what we have, fostering a positive mindset and enhancing our overall well-being.

THE POWER OF GRATITUDE

Gratitude has the ability to transform our lives. When we deliberately focus on the positive aspects of our lives and express gratitude for them, our perspective shifts, and we become more aware of the abundance that surrounds us. Research has shown that practicing gratitude regularly can lead to increased happiness, improved mental health, and enhanced relationships. Gratitude also has a profound impact on our academic lives. When students practice gratitude, they develop a mindset of abundance and optimism, which can lead to higher motivation, improved focus, and increased academic performance. By appreciating their educational opportunities, supportive teachers, and resources available to them, students can fully embrace the learning process and maximize their potential.

WAYS TO CULTIVATE GRATITUDE

Cultivating gratitude and appreciation is a skill that can be learned and practiced. Here are some strategies to incorporate gratitude into your daily life as a student:

1. Keep a Gratitude Journal

Start a gratitude journal and write down three things you are grateful for each day. These could be small moments of joy, acts of kindness, or accomplishments. By actively reflecting on and documenting your blessings, you train your mind to focus on the positive aspects of your life.

2. Practice Gratitude Exercises

Engage in gratitude exercises such as writing thank-you notes to people who have positively impacted your life, keeping a gratitude jar where you store notes about moments of gratitude, or simply expressing gratitude verbally to yourself or others. These practices reinforce the habit of recognizing and appreciating the good in your life.

3. Engage in Mindful Appreciation

Take the time to be fully present and appreciate the beauty and wonder of the world around you. Notice the small details in nature, savor your meals, or engage in activities that bring you joy. By practicing mindfulness and appreciating the present moment, you cultivate gratitude for the simple pleasures in life.

4. Seek Perspective

When faced with challenges or setbacks, intentionally seek out different perspectives. Reflect on the lessons you can learn from difficult situations, and find gratitude for the growth and resilience you are developing. This helps shift your mindset from one of adversity to one of gratitude for the opportunities presented through challenges.

5. Express Gratitude to Others

Take the time to show appreciation to the people who support and encourage you. Write heartfelt thank-you notes to your teachers, friends, family, or mentors. Expressing gratitude not only strengthens your relationships but also cultivates a sense of positivity and connection in your life.

THE RIPPLE EFFECT OF GRATITUDE

Practicing gratitude not only enhances your personal well-being but also creates a ripple effect in your environment. When you consistently express gratitude and appreciation, you inspire and uplift those around you. Your positive energy can motivate and encourage your peers, creating a supportive and harmonious atmosphere that enhances everyone's academic journey. Remember, cultivating gratitude and appreciation is a practice that requires consistency and intention. By incorporating these strategies into your daily life as a student, you can develop a mindset of gratitude that will contribute to your happiness, academic success, and overall well-being. So, embrace the power of gratitude and let it transform your life and the lives of those around you. Next up, in Chapter 23, we will discuss the importance of nurturing a positive environment for academic and personal growth.

Chapter 23: Nurturing a Positive Environment

Creating a positive environment is essential for a student's overall well-being and academic success. The environment plays a significant role in shaping an individual's mindset, motivation, and attitude towards learning. Nurturing a positive environment involves cultivating supportive relationships, fostering a sense of belonging, and creating an atmosphere that promotes growth and positivity. In this chapter, we will explore practical strategies to create and maintain a positive environment that enhances students' happiness and academic journey.

UNDERSTANDING THE IMPACT OF ENVIRONMENT

The environment encompasses both the physical surroundings and the people we interact with on a daily basis. It can influence our thoughts, emotions, and behaviors, which in turn shape our overall experiences. Research has shown that a positive environment can lead to improved well-being, increased motivation, and better academic performance. When students are surrounded by positivity, they feel more supported and encouraged. This, in turn, boosts their confidence, self-belief, and resilience. On the other hand, a negative or toxic environment can have detrimental effects, including increased stress, anxiety, and decreased motivation.

CULTIVATING SUPPORTIVE RELATIONSHIPS

One of the most significant factors in creating a positive environment is fostering supportive relationships. Strong relationships with peers, teachers, mentors, and family members provide a sense of belonging and support. These relationships act as a safety net during challenging times, offering guidance, encouragement, and a listening ear. To cultivate supportive relationships: 1. Foster open communication: Encourage open and honest communication among students, teachers, and parents. Create a safe space where individuals can express their thoughts, concerns, and ideas without fear of judgment. 2. Practice active listening: Actively listen and show empathy towards others. Hear their perspectives, validate their feelings, and respond with care and understanding. This creates a supportive atmosphere where individuals feel heard and valued. 3. Offer help and support: Be willing to offer help and support to others. Whether it's assisting with school work, providing emotional support, or cheering each other on, small acts of kindness can go a long way in creating a positive environment. 4. Resolve conflicts constructively: Conflict is inevitable in any environment, but how we handle it can determine the overall atmosphere. Encourage conflict resolution strategies that promote understanding, compromise, and mutual respect. Teach students effective communication and problem-solving skills to navigate conflicts positively.

CREATING A GROWTH-FOCUSED ATMOSPHERE

To nurture a positive environment, it's crucial to create a growth-focused atmosphere that encourages continuous learning, improvement, and resilience. This mindset shift helps students view challenges as opportunities for growth rather than obstacles. Here's how you can create a growth-focused atmosphere: 1. Emphasize effort and progress: Encourage students to focus on their efforts and progress rather than solely on outcomes. Recognize and celebrate their achievements, whether big or small, to reinforce a growth mindset. 2. Provide constructive feedback: Offer feedback that is specific, constructive, and growth-oriented. Encourage students to see feedback as a tool for improvement and guide them towards setting concrete goals to enhance their skills. 3. Encourage curiosity and exploration: Foster a sense of curiosity by encouraging students to ask questions, explore different perspectives, and engage in critical thinking. Provide opportunities for hands-on learning, problem-solving, and independent exploration.

CREATING A SUPPORTIVE PHYSICAL ENVIRONMENT

The physical environment plays a vital role in shaping a positive atmosphere. An organized, clean, and inviting space can enhance focus, motivation, and overall well-being. Here are some strategies to create a supportive physical environment: 1. Optimize the learning environment: Ensure that the learning space is free from distractions, well-lit, and comfortable. Organize materials, resources, and tools in a way that promotes efficiency and easy access. 2. Personalize the space: Allow students to personalize their learning spaces by displaying artwork, motivational quotes, or items that inspire them. This personal touch can create a sense of ownership and pride in the environment. 3. Utilize technology effectively: Incorporate technology that enhances learning and productivity. Provide access to educational resources, digital tools, and platforms that support collaboration and creativity.

In conclusion

Nurturing a positive environment is crucial for students to thrive and succeed academically and personally. By cultivating supportive relationships, creating a growth-focused atmosphere, and designing a supportive physical environment, students will feel empowered, motivated, and inspired to reach their full potential. With a nurturing and positive environment, students can truly embrace the happiness mindset and achieve success in all areas of their lives. Next up:

CHAPTER 24: OVERCOMING CHALLENGES AND OBSTACLES

Chapter 24: Overcoming Challenges and Obstacles

Life is full of challenges and obstacles, and as a student, you are bound to face many of them on your academic journey. However, it is how you deal with these challenges that will determine your success and personal growth. In this chapter, we will explore strategies for overcoming challenges and obstacles, helping you develop the resilience and mindset necessary to thrive in the face of adversity.

UNDERSTANDING CHALLENGES AND OBSTACLES

Challenges and obstacles can come in various forms. They may be academic, such as difficult coursework or exams, or they could be personal challenges, such as time management issues or external commitments. Whatever the challenge may be, it is important to recognize and acknowledge it. When faced with a challenge or obstacle, it is common to feel overwhelmed, frustrated, or even defeated. However, it is important to remember that challenges are a natural part of life and provide an opportunity for growth and learning. By adopting a positive mindset and seeking solutions, you can overcome these challenges and come out stronger on the other side.

DEVELOPING A PROBLEM-SOLVING MINDSET

A key step in overcoming challenges and obstacles is developing a problem-solving mindset. This mindset involves approaching challenges as opportunities rather than roadblocks and actively seeking out solutions. Here are some strategies to help you develop a problem-solving mindset:

1. Identify the Challenge

The first step in overcoming a challenge is to identify and clearly define it. Take some time to reflect on the specific issue you are facing. What are the obstacles that are hindering your progress? By identifying the challenge, you can start to develop a plan of action.

2. Break It Down

Once you have identified the challenge, break it down into smaller, more manageable tasks. Often, challenges can seem overwhelming when viewed as a whole. By breaking them down into smaller steps, you can tackle them one at a time, making the challenge more manageable.

3. Seek Support

Don't be afraid to reach out for support when facing challenges. Whether it's a teacher, a classmate, or a mentor, seeking support can provide valuable insights and new perspectives. Others may have experienced similar challenges and can offer guidance and encouragement.

4. Explore Different Strategies

There is rarely a one-size-fits-all solution to challenges. Explore different strategies and approaches to find what works best for you. Be open to trying new techniques, seeking advice, and embracing trial and error. By being flexible and adaptive, you can find creative solutions that can lead to success.

MAINTAINING RESILIENCE

In addition to developing a problem-solving mindset, maintaining resilience is crucial when facing challenges and obstacles. Resilience is the ability to bounce back from difficult situations and setbacks. Here are some strategies to help you build and maintain resilience:

1. Practice Self-Care

Taking care of your physical, mental, and emotional well-being is vital when facing challenges. Make sure to prioritize self-care activities, such as getting enough sleep, eating nutritious food, engaging in regular physical exercise, and practicing relaxation techniques. Taking care of yourself will help you stay strong and focused during challenging times.

2. Cultivate a Supportive Network

Having a supportive network of friends, family, teachers, and mentors can provide you with the encouragement and guidance you need when facing obstacles. Surround yourself with positive influences who believe in your abilities and can offer support and advice when needed.

3. Reflect and Learn

Every challenge or obstacle presents an opportunity for growth and learning. Take the time to reflect on your experiences, both successful and challenging. What did you learn from the situation? How can you apply that knowledge in the future? By reflecting on past challenges, you can gain valuable insights that will help you navigate future obstacles.

4. Celebrate Small Victories

When facing a significant challenge, it can be easy to become overwhelmed or discouraged. Celebrate small victories along the way to keep yourself motivated and engaged. Recognize and acknowledge your progress, no matter how small it may be. This will help boost your confidence and provide the momentum needed to overcome bigger challenges.

CONCLUSION

Overcoming challenges and obstacles is an essential part of the student experience. By developing a problem-solving mindset, maintaining resilience, and seeking support, you can navigate through challenging times and emerge stronger and more resilient. Remember, challenges are opportunities for growth, and with the right mindset, you can overcome any obstacle that comes your way. Stay focused, stay positive, and never give up.

Chapter 25: Sustaining the Happiness Mindset for Success

The journey towards a happiness mindset does not end once it is developed. Sustaining this mindset is essential for long-term success and well-being. In this final chapter, we will explore strategies and practices to help students maintain their happiness mindset and thrive in all areas of their lives.

1. REFLECTING ON PROGRESS

Regularly taking time to reflect on your progress is important for sustaining a happiness mindset. Reflecting allows you to acknowledge your achievements, recognize areas for improvement, and stay motivated. Set aside time each week to review your goals, accomplishments, and challenges faced. Celebrate your successes, no matter how small they may seem, and use any setbacks or failures as learning opportunities.

2. CULTIVATING RESILIENCE

Resilience is key to sustaining a happiness mindset. Life will always bring challenges and setbacks, but it is how you respond to them that matters. Cultivating resilience involves developing the ability to adapt, bounce back, and learn from difficult situations. Practice self-compassion, recognize your strengths, and focus on finding solutions rather than dwelling on problems. Surround yourself with supportive people who can provide guidance and encouragement during challenging times.

3. MAINTAINING SELF-CARE PRACTICES

Self-care should be a priority in your daily routine to sustain a happiness mindset. Take care of your physical, emotional, and mental well-being by getting enough sleep, eating nutritious meals, and engaging in regular exercise. Make time for activities that bring you joy and relaxation, such as hobbies, spending time in nature, or practicing mindfulness and meditation. Remember to set boundaries and say no when necessary to avoid burnout.

4. SEEKING GROWTH AND LEARNING OPPORTUNITIES

Continuing to seek growth and learning opportunities is essential for sustaining a happiness mindset. Challenge yourself to step out of your comfort zone, acquire new knowledge and skills, and pursue personal growth. Engage in lifelong learning through courses, workshops, reading, or online resources. Embrace failure as a natural part of the learning process and view setbacks as opportunities for growth and improvement.

5. CULTIVATING A POSITIVE SUPPORT NETWORK

Surrounding yourself with positive and supportive individuals is crucial for sustaining a happiness mindset. Seek out friendships and relationships that uplift and inspire you. Engage in meaningful conversations, offer support to others, and create a network of individuals who share similar values and goals. Remember that it is okay to distance yourself from negative influences and toxic relationships that drain your energy and undermine your happiness.

6. PRACTICING GRATITUDE

Gratitude is a powerful tool for sustaining a happiness mindset. Incorporate a daily gratitude practice into your routine by taking a few moments each day to reflect on what you are grateful for. Write down three things you appreciate or verbally express your gratitude to someone who has made a positive impact on your life. Cultivating gratitude helps shift your focus towards the positive aspects of your life and fosters a sense of contentment and happiness.

7. EMBRACING CHALLENGES WITH A GROWTH MINDSET

Maintaining a growth mindset is essential for sustaining a happiness mindset. Embrace challenges as opportunities for growth and learning. Rather than seeing obstacles as roadblocks, view them as stepping stones towards success. Develop a belief in your ability to learn and improve, and approach challenges with optimism and perseverance. Remember that setbacks are temporary and that you have the power to overcome them.

8. INSPIRING AND SUPPORTING OTHERS

One of the best ways to sustain a happiness mindset is by inspiring and supporting others. Share your knowledge, experiences, and successes with those around you. Offer encouragement and guidance to individuals who may be facing challenges or setbacks. By uplifting others, you create a positive ripple effect that not only benefits them but also reinforces your own happiness mindset.

CONCLUSION

Sustaining a happiness mindset requires consistent effort, reflection, and practice. By incorporating these strategies into your daily life, you can continue to thrive academically and personally. Remember that happiness is not a destination but a journey, and by nurturing a positive mindset, you can experience long-term success, well-being, and fulfillment.

Printed by Amazon Italia Logistica S.r.l.
Torrazza Piemonte (TO), Italy

57632458R00085